This Is the Way We Eat Our Food

By Laine Falk

Children's Press®
An Imprint of Scholastic Inc.
New York Toronto London Auckland Sydney
Mexico City New Delhi Hong Kong
Danbury, Connecticut

These content vocabulary word builders are for grades 1–2.

Subject Consultant: Eli J. Lesser, MA, Director of Education, National Constitution Center, Philadelphia, Pennsylvania

Reading Consultant: Cecilia Minden-Cupp, PhD, Early Literacy Consultant and Author, Chapel Hill, North Carolina

Photographs © 2010: Alamy Images: back cover, 1, 19 bottom left (Corbis Premium RF), 10 (JTB Photo Communications, Inc.), 5 bottom left (JupiterImages/Pixland), 15, 21 right center (Philip Quirk), 11, 21 left center (Sean Sprague); Corbis Images/Annie Griffiths Belt: 16, 21 right, 23 bottom; Getty Images: 20 right center (Jenny Acheson), 13, 21 left (James Baigrie), cover (Paul Burns), 8, 22 center (C Squared Studios), 9, 20 left center (Shannon Fagan), 17, 22 bottom (JupiterImages), 19 top right (Alex Mares-Manton), 5 bottom right (Jose Luis Pelaez), 5 top right (Camille Tokerud), 2, 19 top left, 20 left (Roger Tully); iStockphoto: 6 (Yuriy Afonkin), 19 bottom right (Keith Eddleman), 12, 22 top (Jeanell Norvell), 14, 23 top (Malcolm Romain), 5 top left (Francisco Romero), 7, 20 right (Scott Vickers). Map 20-21: Jim McMahon

Art Direction and Production: Scholastic Classroom Magazines

Library of Congress Cataloging-in-Publication Data

Falk, Laine, 1974-
This is the way we eat our food / Laine Falk.
   p. cm.
Includes bibliographical references and index.
ISBN 13: 978-0-531-21339-1 (lib. bdg.) 978-0-531-21439-8 (pbk.)
ISBN 10: 0-531-21339-0 (lib. bdg.) 0-531-21439-7 (pbk.)
1. Food–Juvenile literature. 2. Food habits–Juvenile literature. 3. Cookery, International–Juvenile literature. I. Title.
TX355.F36 2009   641.3–dc22 2009010972

©2010 Scholastic Inc.
All rights reserved. Published in 2010 by Children's Press, an imprint of Scholastic Inc.
Published simultaneously in Canada. Printed in China.   62
SCHOLASTIC, CHILDREN'S PRESS, and associated logos are trademarks and/or registered trademarks of Scholastic Inc.
2 3 4 5 6 7 8 9 10 R 18 17 16 15 14 13 12 11 10

CONTENTS

How Do You Eat Your Food? 4–5

Eating With Tools 6–13

Eating With Hands 14–19

Kids Around the World Eat 20–21

Your New Words 22–23

Index 24

Find Out More 24

Meet the Author 24

How Do You Eat Your Food?

Do you eat pizza with your hands? Do you sip soup from a spoon?

Children around the world eat in different ways. Let's see how they eat!

These children eat
in the United States.

Eating With Tools

You may use a **fork** when you eat. People in many parts of the world do.

It would be hard to eat spaghetti without a fork!

fork

This girl eats spaghetti with a fork in Italy.

7

In some places, people do not use forks as much. They may use **chopsticks**.

People use chopsticks to pick up small pieces of food. They use them to pick up noodles and tiny grains of rice.

chopsticks

This boy eats with chopsticks in Japan.

Bread can also be a tool for eating. Here, people use pieces of soft, flat bread to pick up their food. Then they eat the bread and the food together.

bread

These boys use bread to pick up their food in Ethiopia.

In some places, a **banana leaf** might be used instead of a plate. When you have finished eating, you don't have to wash the dishes!

banana leaf

This boy in Indonesia holds his food in a banana leaf.

13

Eating With Hands

People in many places use their hands to eat fruit.

It is fun to eat a sweet **mango** with your hands!

mango

This boy eats a mango
with his hands in Australia.

People eat bread with their hands, too. **Pita** is like a pocket of bread. You can put food in the pocket.

Cornmeal cakes are bread made from corn. These are called arepas (ah-RAY-puhz) in Spanish.

pita

This girl makes cornmeal cakes in Colombia.

cornmeal cakes

What kinds of food do you eat with your hands? What tools do you use to eat?

How will you eat *your* food today?

These children eat with their hands in the United States.

19

United States

Colombia

Italy

Ethiopia

KIDS AROUND THE WORLD

Look at this map. Can you match the children in the photos to the countries where they live?

North America

United States

Atlantic Ocean

Colombia

Equator

Pacific Ocean

South America

Compass Rose

North

West — East

South

Indonesia

Israel

Japan

Australia

EAT

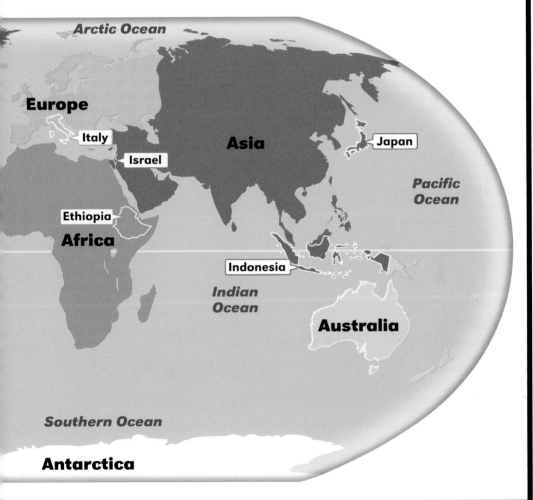

Arctic Ocean

Europe

Italy

Israel

Asia

Japan

Pacific Ocean

Ethiopia

Africa

Indonesia

Indian Ocean

Australia

Southern Ocean

Antarctica

YOUR NEW WORDS

banana leaf (buh-**na**-nuh leef) the large, flat leaf from a banana tree

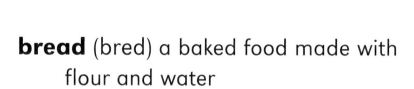

bread (bred) a baked food made with flour and water

chopsticks (**chop**-stiks) thin sticks used to eat food, especially in Asia

cornmeal cakes (**korn**-meel kayks) round, thin patties of bread made from corn. They can be baked, fried, or grilled.

fork (fork) a tool with prongs and a handle used to eat food

mango (**mang**-goh) a sweet, tropical fruit with red, yellow, or green skin

pita (**pee**-tuh) a thin, flat bread that can be used as a pocket to put other food inside

INDEX

Australia, 15, 21

banana leaf, 12
bread, 10, 16

chopsticks, 8
Colombia, 17, 20
cornmeal cakes, 16

Ethiopia, 11, 20

forks, 6, 8
fruit, 14

hands, 4, 14, 16, 18

Indonesia, 13, 21
Italy, 7, 20

Japan, 9, 21

mango, 14

noodles, 8

pita, 16
pizza, 4
plate, 12

rice, 8

soup, 4
spaghetti, 6
spoon, 4

United States, 5, 19, 20

FIND OUT MORE

Book:
Dooley, Norah. *Everybody Cooks Rice*. Minneapolis, Minnesota: Carolrhoda Books, 1992.

Website:
Don't Gross Out the World
http://www.fekids.com/img/kln/flash/DontGrossOutTheWorld.swf

MEET THE AUTHOR
Laine Falk is a writer and Scholastic editor. She lives in New York. She likes to share ice cream cones with her son.